ISRAEL

W9-BMH-568

PALPHOT

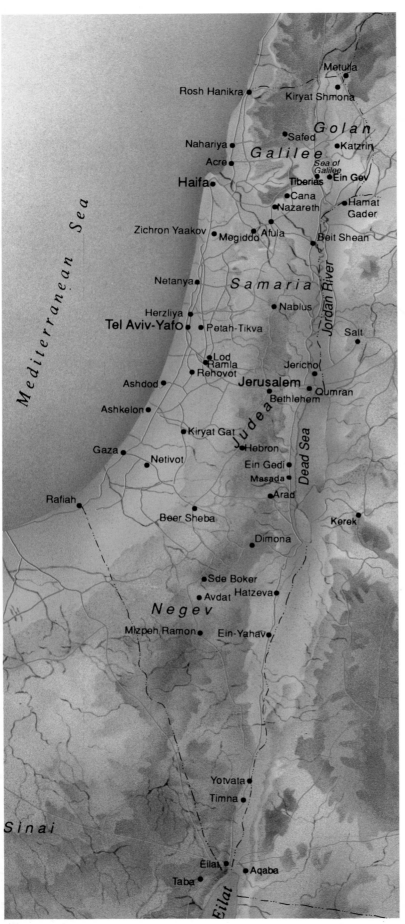

CONTENTS

INTRODUCTION

The history of Israel spans many thousands of years. Bridging Africa, Asia and Europe, crossed by highways and major trade routes, it has always been an important strategic point.

A cradle of mankind, history can be traced back to the Bronze Age. First the Patriarchs and then King Saul lived peaceful lives in the land - until they became victims of the persecution of the Semitic peoples. Jerusalem was made the capital of the kingdom under the rule of King David. The building of the Second Temple, the Roman Conquest, the Crusades, and finally the Zionist movement are all part of the turbulent history of Israel, until the State was established on 15th May 1948.

The ranks of the new Israeli citizens were quietly swelled by the arrival of Jewish immigrants who streamed in from the neighbouring Arab countries - anxious to return to their homeland.

A modern miracle occurred as these people were settled, cared for and trained to take their place in the new state.

Their totally different ethnic backgrounds and cultures have now blended together in the melting pot of Israeli life.

Each community however, retains its special arts, dress and customs, proudly keeping these traditions alive.

Hopes for the long awaited tranquility in this troubled area have never really been completely fulfilled. Negotiations frequently take place and all hope that the fervent desire for a complete and lasting peace may one day be realized.

Turning to the land itself, it is indeed difficult to visualize so much variety in such a small country. Snow-capped mountains, fertile valleys, arid and desolate regions of desert, sparkling lakes and seaside resorts are all to be found within the boundaries of Israel. The hustle and bustle of towns, noisy local markets, the sanctity of the holy places and a close association with the Bible all wait to be experienced by travellers of all ages and interests from all walks of life.

JERUSALEM

Jerusalem, city of a hundred names and a thousand faces, holy to Judaism, Christianity and Islam is undoubtedly the jewel in the crown that is Israel. Abraham's near sacrifice of Isaac on Mt. Moriah, David's establishment of the small Jebusite town as his capital and Solomon's construction of the Temple enshrined Jerusalem in the hearts of Jews. Throughout the nineteen centuries since the destruction of the temple and the exile, Jews the world over pray in the direction of Jerusalem. Christians connect Jerusalem with the last years in the life of Jesus. Here he taught, was arrested, crucified and resurrected. Moslems associate Jerusalem with El Aksa, the point from which Mohammed ascended to the Seventh Heaven. After Mecca and Medina, Jerusalem is Islam's third holiest city. Jerusalem sanctity and mysticisim have inspired prophets, artists, poets and scholars for centuries. But it has also become a major cultural centre with museums, galleries, theatres and also universities and yeshivot. The presence of the su-

preme legislative administrative and judicial bodies have made it into a modern capital. Sophisticated stores compete with oriental bazaars for the attention of shoppers. The variety of costumes which rub shoulders in its streets — Hassidic capotas, Moslem jalabiyas, dozens of different monks' robes, denim jeans and many, many more — can only be matched by the infinite motives which move people to inhabit or visit Jerusalem. The harmony of church bells, the muezzin's call to prayers, communal study in yeshivot and dealers offering their wares all combine in the setting for this cosmopolitan city.

THE GATES

There are eight gates in the Old City walls.
The Damascus Gate - which is the most ornate, is

considered by many to be the most beautiful. It was built by Suleiman the Great in 1537. The road to Damascus used to start here.

The New Gate - is the only gate that was not built by Suleiman. It was opened in 1887 to facilitate passage from the Christian Quarter to the Catholic institutions outside the walls.

The Jaffa Gate - this was the starting point of the road to Jaffa, an important port town, and so an outlet for trade.

Zion Gate - connects the Armenian Quarter with Mount Zion. It has also been called the "Jewish Quarter Gate" because of its proximity to the Jewish Quarter.

The Dung Gate - this is the nearest gate to the Western Wall. It is low and narrow - just wide enough to permit the passage of a man and his donkey. Much of the city's refuse is taken to the Kidron Valley by an ancient sewer which runs beneath this gate.

The Golden Gate - is situated in the east wall of the Temple Mount enclosure. It is sometimes also called the Gate of Mercy. The gate was sealed many years ago by the Turks. Jewish tradition holds that the Messiah will enter Jerusalem through this gate.

The Lions' Gate - is named after the pair of lions who guard it. The gate is also known as St. Stephen's Gate; according to tradition he was martyred nearby.

Herod's Gate - is named for a mistaken identification of a church nearby as the home of Herod Antipas. Decorated with a roselike design, it is called in Hebrew "The Gate of the Flowers". It was closed until 1875.

1. *Jaffa Gate*
2. *The Golden Gate*
3. *Lion's Gate*
4. *Dung Gate*
5. *Herod's Gate*
6. *Zion Gate*
7. *The New Gate*
8. *Damascus Gate*
9. *Jerusalem's ramparts*

THE CITADEL

On the western side of the Old City the massive structure of the Citadel looms large and overpowering. It stands on the site where Herod built his palace at the end of the first Century B.C. The enormous stones comprise some of Herod's most impressive and important fortifications. Only this part of the city walls remained intact after the destruction of Jerusalem by the Romans.

The Tower of Phasael, just inside the Jaffa Gate, is a Jerusalem landmark to this day. From the roof of this tower there is a wonderful view of the Old City. Flights of steps lead to the walkway which runs round the top of the Old City walls. This rampart walk has been divided into four routes, and each one provides a breathtaking view of the Old City of Jerusalem.

The Museum houses a permanent collection of ethnic costumes relating to the city. Models show the structure of the buildings, whilst a multi-screen slide show brings to life the historical aspects. During the summer months visitors can enjoy an audio-visual presentation, when the very stones seem to come alive at the excitement of the pomp and ceremony of the story of Jerusalem being told.

Below: The Citadel during a Sound and Light Show

Views of the Citadel

The Western Wall showing the path leading to the Temple Mount and the Dome of the Rock

In the Western Wall tunnels

Opposite: *Prayers and festivities by the Western Wall*

ARCHAEOLOGY AND EXCAVATIONS

The southern and western wall excavations adjoining the El-Aksa Mosque have revealed many interesting features of the construction of the city. The remains of the huge Robinson Arch can clearly be seen. It is now believed that a staircase from this arch led to Herod's Basilica. These gates were used by Herod when he entered the city. Wilson's Arch connected the Temple to the Upper City.

An archaeological park has been laid out along the southern wall of the Temple. Easy paths and plaques with clear explanations make walking here an enjoyable and informative way of spending leisure time.

Previous page
Above right: *Prayers with Father*
Below: *Service in Wilson's Arch*
Opposite page: *The excavated stairway leading to the Temple Mount*
Below: *The archaeological park. There are plaques with clearly marked explanations at many points along the broad paths.*

THE WESTERN WALL

The Western Wall is all that remains of the Second Temple. Pilgrims gather from all over the world to pray at this sacred shrine. The great Herodian stones rest one on top of the other without cement between them to hold them in place. More than half of the wall is below the present day ground level.

During the years that Jerusalem was controlled by the Jordanians (from 1948-1967) access to the Wall was forbidden. After the reunification in June 1967 the site was cleared, the crowded hovels around it were pulled down, and a vast paved plaza was constructed. This has now become a meeting place for communal prayer and many public celebrations. The Western Wall is never deserted. At any hour of the day or night, winter or summer, one can always find Jews there, standing in front of the Wall in devout prayer - or placing their messages in the cracks and crevices between the stones.

THE OLD CITY

The Old City of Jerusalem - is composed of four quarters, each with its own distinctive characteristics. The Christian Quarter is in the north-west; the Moslem Quarter in the north-east; the Armenian Quarter in the south-west, and the Jewish Quarter in the south-east.

These four quarters, covering an area of approximately 850 dunams, are surrounded by the city walls. Built of huge blocks of grey stone, the present walls were constructed between 1536 and 1539 during the time of Suleiman the Magnificent.

THE JEWISH QUARTER

Excavations in the Jewish Quarter have revealed untold treasures. Parts of the wide colonnaded street, the Cardo Maximus, have been uncovered. This was once the main thoroughfare of the Roman-Byzantine city. A mosaic map of sixth century Jerusalem was found in Jordan in 1884. This portrays the colonnaded streets and buildings of the time; it is known as the Madaba Map. A replica can be seen today at the beginning of the Cardo. Byzantine and Crusader remains in the reconstructed Cardo have been incorporated into the modern structures which now stand on the original paving stones.

There is much evidence of the way in which the Jews lived in Jerusalem until the destruction of the Second Temple. The Burnt House, which contains relics of one of the priestly families, is all that remains of the homes in the Upper City which were razed by the Romans in 70 C.E. Remains of Israelite walls and an Israelite tower have also been found. After the victory of Saladin in 1187, life for the Jews became easier. Synagogues and centres of learning were built - and then destroyed once again during the Jordanian occupation of Jerusalem from 1948-1967.

Today the Jewish Quarter contains reconstructed synagogues and yeshivot - together with modern apartment buildings and houses. All are tastefully built around paved courtyards and well kept gardens - the old and the new blending together in a delightful fashion.

Above: One of the Sephardi synagogues in the Jewish Quarter of the Old City
Below: Part of the restored Byzantine Cardo, in the Jewish Quarter of the Old City.
Opposite: The Old City Wall - archaeological park, the reconstructed Jewish Quarter and the Temple Mount. In the background, the Mount of Olives

The Golden Menorah in the Cardo
The first golden seven-branched Menorah made since the destruction of the Temple, by the Temple Institute, Jerusalem (Donated by Vadim Rabinovitz)

THE TEMPLE MOUNT

For the three major monotheistic religions, the Temple Mount is the historical and spiritual focus of Jerusalem. It is revered by Jews as the holiest place on earth. The rock at the centre of the Temple Mount (now covered by the Dome of the Rock) is the place where Abraham prepared to sacrifice his son, Isaac. Solomon built the First Temple here, and later the Second Temple was erected on the same spot. Christianity associates the Temple Mount with the preaching of Jesus, whilst for Moslems this is the accepted place from which Mohammed ascended to heaven.

THE POOL OF SILWAN

Silwan, just outside the Old City walls, runs along the Ophel down to the Kidron Valley. This was the site picked by David for the establishment of his capital, Jerusalem, 5,000 years ago.

The Pool of Silwan receives water from the Spring of Gihon by way of Hezekiah's Tunnel. Since the sole source of water for Jerusalem was from this spring, it was imperative to conceal and divert the course in times of war. This was achieved with such success that it was not until the 15th century that the residents of Jerusalem learned that the Pool of Silwan was not the water source.

Previous page 18
Above: The reconstructed Hurva Synagogue
Below: The Cardo
Previous page 19
Silwan - the City of David
Inset: The Archaeological Walk in section "G" of the excavations at the City of David
Above: The Pool of Silwan in the City of David.
Built by King Hezekiah, this pool, quarried out of the rocks, was where Jesus sent the blind man to wash.
Below: Hezekiah's workers cut the tunnel through the rock in order to bring the waters of the Gihon Spring inside the city walls in times of siege.
Opposite: The Dome of the Rock
This magnificent mosque was built on the site of the First and Second Temples in 691 A.D. by the Omayad Khalif, Abd El Malik ibn Mirwan.

THE DOME OF THE ROCK

One of the wonders of the modern world, the gold-capped Dome of the Rock is an outstanding landmark of Jerusalem. Wall mosaics, beautiful carpets and stained glass windows inside the mosque vie with the marble facade and blue and gold tiles on the outside walls of the building.

Opposite Above: "Solomon's Stables" - part of the foundations of the Second Temple which were used by the Crusaders to house their horses.
Opposite Below: The interior of the El-Aqsa Mosque

Below: The Cupola of the Dome of the Rock. Red and gold stucco painting decorate the wood-lined cupola. A great chain hangs from the centre - all that remains of the silver candelabra that once graced the beautiful mosque.

THE EL-AQSA MOSQUE

This mosque stands over an underground building called the Ancient Arcade. Built between 709-715 A.D. by Caliph Waleed, the son of Abd El Malik, the silver domed mosque is easily recognized on the southern part of the Temple Mount.

Exquisitely decorated pillars and arches support the roof; priceless rugs cover the floor. During the time of the Crusaders the mosque was used as a residence for the knights in charge of the Temple area. These knights became known as the Templars. Saladin restored the building to its original use as a mosque after the defeat of the Crusaders.

SOLOMON'S STABLES

To the east of the El-Aqsa Mosque, a flight of steps in the paved courtyard leads to the underground vaults of Solomon's Stables. In 1099 the Crusaders kept their horses here.

MARKETS

Every visitor to Jerusalem is fascinated by the bazaars and markets of the Old City. There are unlimited possibilities for bargaining. The incredible array of spices, sweetmeats, fruits and vegetables all remind the tourist that the atmosphere of the Middle East is totally different to anything that he may have encountered "at home".

Stalls and stores display antiques, pottery, jewellery, carved olive wood objects, embroideries and leather work. The list is endless - there is something to suit all tastes, and all pockets. Nobody needs to go away without a souvenir of his visit to Jerusalem.

THE VIA DOLOROSA

The Way of the Cross commemorates the path which Jesus walked bearing the cross from the Place of Judgement (Praetorium) to Calvary.

Every Friday, led by Franciscan monks, groups of Christian pilgrims from around the world, retrace these steps, starting at the Church of the Flagellation and ending at the Church of the Holy Sepulchre.

There are fourteen stations along Christendom's most sacred route - each one marks an event that took place during the last walk before the Crucifixion. Nine of these points are actually along the Via Dolorosa, and five are inside the Church of the Holy Sepulchre.

Opposite: *Scenes in the markets of the Old City of Jerusalem*

Above right: *Prayers outside the Third Station of the Via Dolorosa*

Below: *The courtyard of the First Station of the Cross. Here pilgrims gather every Friday to trace the path of the Stations of the Cross*

Overleaf P. 26

Above left: *Outside the Fifth Station of the Cross where Simon of Cyrene helped Jesus carry the cross*

Above right: *Outside the Ninth Station of the Cross, where Jesus fell for the third time. A column built into the doorway of the Coptic Church marks the site.*

Below: *The Church of the Flagellation - the Second Station of the Cross.*

Overleaf, p.27 Above right: *The Fourth Station of the Cross, The Church of Our Lady of the Spasm, where the Virgin Mary, the mother of Jesus, met Him carrying the cross*

Above left: *The Chapel of the Second Station of the Cross*

Below right: *Part of the pavement in the courtyard of the Antonia Fortress, the remains of which are to be found in the Convent of the Sisters of Sion*

Below left: *The Stone of Basilindia. Markings on the pavement are evidence of the "King's Game" played by the Roman legionnaires.*

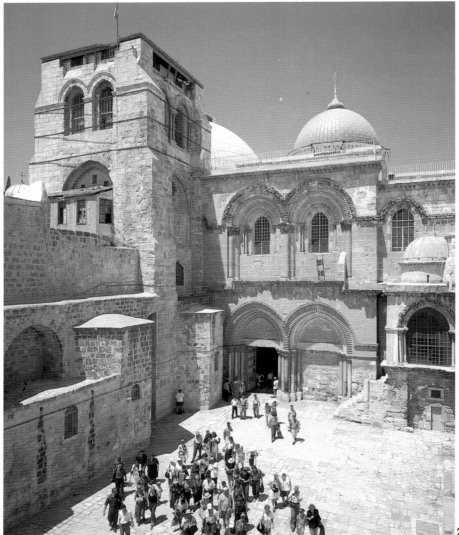

1. *The Church of the Holy Sepulchre*

2. *Interior of the Tomb of Jesus*

3. *The central dome of the Catholicon, supported by the high Crusader arches*

4. *Calvary, the Eleventh Station, where Jesus is nailed to the Cross.*

THE CHURCH OF THE HOLY SEPULCHRE

Venerated by many Christians as one of the holiest of their shrines, the Church of the Holy Sepulchre terminates the way of the Via Dolorosa. It is believed that Jesus was crucified on this spot, and here we find the tomb of Jesus.

In 325 A.D. the Emperor Constantine the Great ordered a church to be erected on this spot. His mother, the Empress Helena, discovered the tomb of Jesus after the place was revealed to her in a dream.

Three different buildings were erected - a round church, the Anastasis above the empty grave of Jesus; a basilica, the Martyrium; and the square between the two churches a shrine marking the place of the crucifixion - Calvarium (Golgotha).

In 614 A.D. these buildings were destroyed by the Persians. They were rebuilt and destroyed once more in 1009 A.D. by Caliph Hakim. Once again they were partially restored - until the Crusaders erected the present church in 1149 A.D. after their conquest of Jerusalem. Now the tomb of Jesus and the place of crucifixion are under one roof.

Below: *The interior of the Church of the Holy Sepulchre*

MOUNT OF OLIVES

The Mount of Olives nearby holds an important place in Christianity. It was here that Jesus taught His disciples during His mission in Jerusalem - here He was made a prisoner, here He wept for Jerusalem, and here He is believed to have ascended to heaven.

The Church of all Nations with its ornately decorated facade glinting in the sunlight, and the Garden of Gethsemane with its grove of ancient olive trees dating back to Byzantine times and cared for today by the Franciscan Brotherhood are important holy sites for visitors.

The village of Bethany, now known as El-Azariah, is famed as the place where Jesus performed the miracle of the raising of Lazarus four days after his death. A steep flight of steps leads to the tomb which is inside a cave. A minaret of a Moslem mosque today stands on the site of the cave.

Below: *The Church of St. Anne, Bethesda. In the foreground are the excavations of the Pool of Five Colonnades - known as the Pool of Bethesda*

Opposite: *The Church of All Nations - Gethsemane. Amidst the trees is the Russian Orthodox Church of Mary Magdalene*

THE KIDRON VALLEY

It is believed in Jewish tradition that the Messiah will come from the east, pass the Mount of Olives and continue through the Kidron Valley before arriving at the Temple Mount. All those who have died will rise on that day to escort the Messiah into the city. During the period of the First Temple, impressive burial chambers were carved into the rocks, testimony to the importance of the area. They can still be seen today.

Above: The Kidron Valley - from the left Absalom's Pillar, the Tomb of St. James and the Tomb of Zacharias. In the background, the Mount of Olives

Below right: An ancient olive tree in the Garden of Gethsemane
Opposite:
Above left: The Church of Dominus Flevit - "The Lord Wept". The church on the slopes of the Mount of Olives faces the Temple Mount. The present church is built on the site of the ancient church. It marks the spot where Jesus wept over the approaching destruction of Jerusalem.
Above right: Bethany - the Church of St. Lazarus
Below right: The Church of the Tomb of the Virgin Mary. Built by the Crusaders, this church contains the tomb of the Virgin Mary.
Below left: The Chapel of the Ascension - marking the traditional spot where Jesus ascended to heaven

THE CHURCH OF ST. PETER IN GALLICANTU

The church, built in 1931, stands on the accepted site of the House of Caiaphas, the High Priest at the time of the arrest of Jesus. Traditionally it is believed that this is the place where Peter denied his master.

At the time of the Second Temple, steps in the courtyard of the Church of St. Peter in Gallicantu connected the City of David with the Upper City (Mt. Zion). This stairway can still be seen - excavations have revealed inscriptions and weights and measures of Second Temple times, as well as a rock-cut flagellation post.

1. The Church of St. Peter in Gallicantu
2. The mosaic-adorned interior of the Church

3. An ancient flight of stairs leading up to the Church, believed to be those trodden by Jesus on his way to trial

THE GARDEN TOMB

The tranquility and beauty of the grounds of the Garden Tomb make this site a truly meaningful place of pilgrimage for the many visitors who pass through its doors on a visit to the Holy Land.

The site was discovered by a group of British Christians. Archaeological evidence of the two-roomed Herodian tomb, the huge, deep cistern, and the skull-shaped hill, as detailed in the New Testament, all led them to believe this to be the possible site of the crucifixion and the Resurrection of Jesus.

The Garden Tomb Association, with headquarters in London, was founded in 1893. To this day the administration of the Garden Tomb is carried out by this evangelical foundation.

Above: *Golgotha - the hill near which the Garden Tomb is situated. Charles Gordon believed this to be Golgotha because of the resemblance of the hill to a human skull.*
Below: *The Garden Tomb - this site, north of the Damascus Gate, outside the walls of Jerusalem, is believed by many Protestants to be the place of the Crucifixion and the Resurrection of Jesus.*

MOUNT ZION

Overlooking the Sultan's Pool, Mount Zion has always been an important point of interest for visitors to Jerusalem. Some of the shrines most sacred to Christianity and Judaism are to be found here. The black-coned roof of the Dormition Abbey stands out against the Jerusalem skyline. Traditionally it is believed that the death of Mary occurred here.

Close by is the Cenacle or Coenaculum - the Hall of the Last Supper. Jesus and his followers celebrated the Passover feast here. Beneath the Cenacle is the Hall of the Washing of the Feet, a small room which leads into a fair sized hall housing the Tomb of King David. Although it is quite possible that this is not the true grave, it nevertheless became a hallowed place for pilgrims between 1948 and 1967 when the Western Wall was in Jordanian hands and could not be visited by Jews.

opposite: above right: The Dormition Abbey by moonlight

Above left: Bird's eye view of Mt. Zion

Below right: The traditional Tomb of King David. Pious Jews still come to pray at the tomb, although in fact King David is probably buried elsewhere.

Below left: A wood and ivory effigy of the Virgin Mary on her deathbed in the crypt of the Church of the Dormition.

Below: The Cenacle - the hall of the Last Supper - in the Dormition Abbey

WEST JERUSALEM

The tall tower of the West Jerusalem Y.M.C.A. provides an excellent point to view both the Old City and the New City. Many first class hotels can be seen nearby. West Jerusalem has developed and expanded enormously in recent years. Restaurants, cafes and modern shops in street malls all combine to make "new Jerusalem" an exciting, busy city whose cosmopolitan atmosphere is unique. Important new buildings, constructed from Jerusalem stone, blend into their surroundings, whilst the well-kept parks and gardens play an important part in beautifying the city. Universities, synagogues, museums, libraries and galleries provide cultural stimulation. All offer a wide range of lectures, concerts and exhibitions on contemporary and classical themes to suit all ages and interests. The new suburbs of Jerusalem which started to appear after 1976 are a far cry from the original garden suburbs founded by German immigrants in the 1920s.

Overleaf p. 38: Bird's eye view of the western section of Jerusalem. In the foreground, Montefiore's Windmill and Yemin Moshe. In the background, some of Jerusalem's leading hotels.

THE KNESSET

The seat of the Israeli Parliament, the Knesset, moved to its present location in 1966. Its sessions, three times a week, are open to the public.

The long, low building of pink Jerusalem stone was designed by Joseph Klarwein and Dov Karmi. It contains many impressive works of art. Three magnificent tapestries by Marc Chagall hang in the reception hall, and he also designed the floor and wall mosaics. Facilities for the one hundred and twenty Knesset members include a synagogue, reading and conference rooms, a library and a restaurant.

Benno Elkan's menorah, which stands opposite the Knesset, was a gift from Britain to Israel. The menorah is modelled on the seven-branched candelabrum from the Temple which the Jewish exiles carried to Rome. Depicting twenty-nine images from Jewish life and history, it is the official emblem of the State of Israel.

Previous Page
Above: *General view of Ramot, a new suburb of Jerusalem*
Below left: *Mea Shearim - view through an archway*
Below right: *Market scene - Machane Yehuda*
opposite page
Above left: *The Jerusalem Theatre*

Above right: *The Bible Lands Museum*
Below: *The Knesset - Israel's Parliament*
Inset: *The Knesset Menorah - the emblem of the State of Israel*
above: *The Malcha Canyon*
left: *The Great Synagogue, Jerusalem*
right: *Pedestrian mall (Midrahov)*

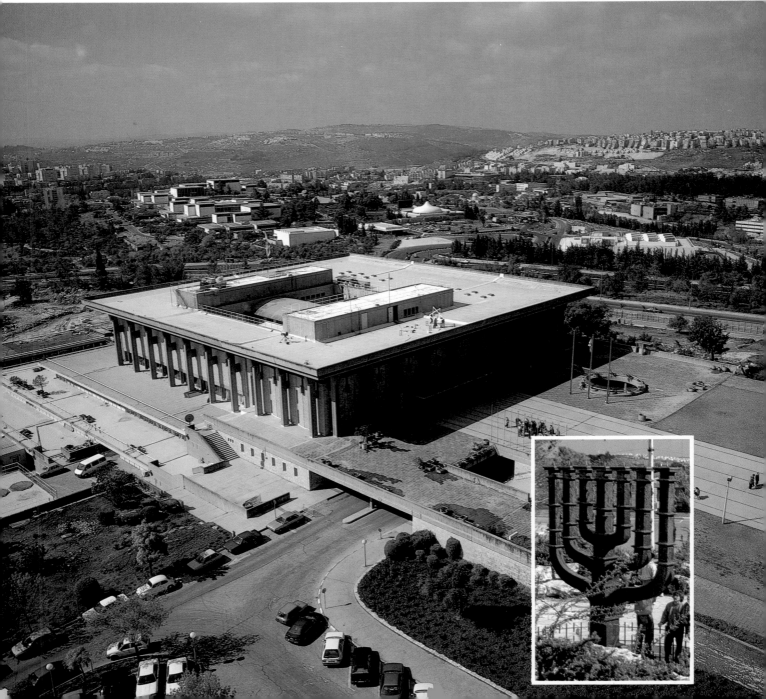

THE ISRAEL MUSEUM

The Israel Museum was opened in 1965. Sections are devoted to Judaica, archaeology and ethnic collections. The exhibitions, both permanent and temporary, of drawings, paintings and sculpture of modern Israeli artists are constantly being updated and enlarged. There is a full programme of lectures, concerts and films. The youth wing is always filled with crowds of youngsters, all eager to learn and participate in the activities offered by this vibrant part of the museum.

THE SHRINE OF THE BOOK

The Shrine of the Book is perhaps the most important part of the museum. It contains the priceless biblical manuscripts which were found in 1947 in caves at Qumran. A special building was erected to house the precious scrolls. The domed white exterior resembles the lid of one of the earthenware jars in which the scrolls were hidden; this contrasts starkly with the wall of black basalt nearby. The shrine itself is subterranean, reminiscent of the caves in which the scrolls were found.

YAD VASHEM

The Martyrs' and Heroes' Remembrance Law - Yad Vashem, was passed by the Knesset in August 1953. Near to Mount Herzl, in the western section of Jerusalem, an impressive complex was built to commemorate the victims of the Holocaust. The Hall of Remembrance which contains the Eternal Light is used regularly for ceremonies by visitors who come to pay their respects. The towering Pillar of Heroism honours the resistance fighters. A small synagogue, library and museum are all important components of the complex. The great blocks of stone in the Valley of the Destroyed Communities pay silent homage to the millions who perished, whilst the quiet dignity of the Avenue of the Righteous Gentiles perpetuates the names of non-Jews who were imperilled trying to save their Jewish neighbours.

Opposite:
Above left: Interior of the Shrine of the Book
Above right: The Shrine of the Book at the Israel Museum
Below: The Israel Museum at night
Above: Valley of the Destroyed Communities.
Below: Yad Vashem, the "Ohel Yizkor" Memorial Hall

THE CHAGALL WINDOWS

In 1962 the French Jewish artist, Marc Chagall, presented to the synagogue of the Hadassah-Hebrew University Medical Centre in Ein Karem a set of magnificent stained glass windows. They represent the sons of the Patriarch Jacob from whom the twelve tribes of Israel were later descended. Each tribe has its own symbols - these are portrayed in magnificent colours on the twelve panels. We are told in Genesis 49 that Jacob blessed his sons before his death. Most of the subjects in the windows derive from that story.

THE MODEL OF JERUSALEM AT THE TIME OF THE SECOND TEMPLE

The model, which stands in the grounds of the Holyland Hotel, was built before the reunification of the city. The 1:50 scale model was constructed according to the measurements given in Middot in the Mishnah, and also to fit the description in the histories of Josephus Flavius. The work, using Jerusalem stone, was supervised by Prof. Michael Avi-Yonah. Changes are made in the model when excavations reveal new information. The grandeur of the city can be judged to some extent by this fascinating replica. Every detail is there - the Temple, Herod's Palace, the twin-spired palace of the Hasmoneans, the markets, inns and common dwelling places. It is interesting to compare the Old City of today with Herodian Jerusalem.

Opposite: *Stained glass windows by Marc Chagall*
Above: *The Model of Jerusalem at the time of the Second Temple in the grounds of the Holyland Hotel*

EIN KAREM

Christians identify Ein Karem as the village where the family of John the Baptist lived "in the hill country of Judah" (Luke 1). His birthplace is here. Many of the churches in the surroundings are connected with stories of his life.

BETHLEHEM

Bethlehem is first mentioned in the Bible in Genesis 35:19 - "so Rachel died and she was buried on the way to Ephrath" (that is Bethlehem). The town is situated about 6 km. south of Jerusalem in neatly terraced countryside. The fields east of Bethlehem where shepherds graze their flocks today are accepted as those where Ruth and Boaz met in the fields of Bethlehem. Their union produced Jesse, father of David, who was born in Bethlehem. Later he was annointed as King of Israel by the prophet, Samuel.

One of the holiest sites in Christianity is the manger in Bethlehem where Mary gave birth to Jesus. Helena, mother of Constantine, the Byzantine emperor, built a church in 385 over the site of the manger. Fragments of the mosaic floors of this edifice can still be seen two centuries later.

The Emperor Justinian erected the building as it stands today. The mosaics on the walls, the wax paintings on the columns and the decorations date back to the Crusader period.

Since that time the church has fallen into disrepair. The doorway was lowered by partly sealing the Crusader arch sometime during the seventh century to ensure that Muslims could not enter the church riding their horses. The visitor of today must bend almost double to gain access to the church.

Most religious buildings were destroyed during the Persian invasion of the seventh century A.D., but apparently the Church of the Nativity was saved from desecration - possibly because of the mosaic then on the facade of the church.

Opposite
View of modern Jerusalem

Opposite Below: *The village of Ein Karem*
Below: *Partial view of Bethlehem*

RACHEL'S TOMB

Just ouside Bethlehem, this is the accepted place where Rachel, Jacob's favourite wife, was buried after she died in childbirth "on the road ... to Bethlehem". She is the only biblical matriarch not buried in the family tomb in Hebron. Over the years Rachel's Tomb has become a place of pilgrimage for the Jewish people, especially barren women.

SHEPHERDS' FIELD

To this day shepherds take their flocks to graze in the fields around Bethlehem. The pastoral landscape has changed little since biblical times.

Above left: Rachel's Tomb
Below: Shepherds' Field
Previous p.49
The Church of the Nativity, Bethlehem
Previous p.50
Above left: The silver star of the Grotto of the Nativity
Above right: Interior of the Basilica of the Nativity
Below right: The entrance to the Church of the Nativity
Below left: The grotto of the Nativity.
Opposite: Scenes in the Bethlehem market

HERODIUM

Herod the Great built this fortification in the desert in 37 B.C.E. It stands like the crater of a volcano. In Josephus Flavius' book "Wars of the Jews" he describes in detail this astounding complex. Herod "built round towers all about the top, and filled the remaining space with costly palaces .... He brought a mighty quantity of water from a great distance, and raised an ascent of two hundred steps of the whitest marble". Testifying to this description, remains of the colonnaded halls, the walls painted with frescoes, can still be seen. A classical Roman bath house, one of the earliest synagogues ever found, and huge underground cisterns all helped to create one of the largest and most sumptuous palaces of the Roman Empire.

According to Josephus, Herod died in Jericho in 4 B.C.E. His body was brought to Herodium, but so far, his grave has not been discovered.

Below: *Heodium*
Bird's eye view of the Judean desert

HEBRON

Hebron is one of the oldest and holiest cities in the land. It is associated with the Tomb of the Patriarchs. It is also well known for its glass-blowing industry, and for the grapes, olives and figs that are grown on the terraced hills surrounding the town. Built during the Great Revolt, Hebron was David's capital before Jerusalem.

The Tomb of the Patriarchs is still the most outstanding building in Hebron. The second holiest Jewish shrine, the cave was originally bought by Abraham from Efron the Hittite. Here he buried his wife, Sarah; when he died he was interred close to her. Isaac and Rebecca and Jacob and Leah were all buried there.

Above: *Hebron, the Mosque of Abraham, which was built over the Cave of Machpela, containing the tombs of the Patriarchs*

Below: *The Tombs of Isaac and Rebecca*

Originally Herodian, the present structure was enlarged by the Crusaders and decorated by the Mamelukes. Tombs were built over the graves as Moslems forbade entry into the cave itself.

At present the hall is divided between Jews and Moslems - the larger, more ornate section serves as a mosque, while the smaller, more modest part is used as a synagogue. Visiting hours and times for prayer are also shared.

JERICHO

An evergreen oasis in the Jordan Valley - Jericho, known as the Date City, is 800 feet below sea level. It is thought to be the oldest continuously inhabited city in the world, dating back some 10,000 years.

Jericho was the first town conquered by Joshua after crossing the Jordan. Tel Jericho, opposite Elisha's spring, was the location of Jericho until the Roman period - when it moved to its present site.

Among the most interesting finds is the monumental tower from the Neolithic period. Remnants of a mosaic floor from a sixth century synagogue were also found in Jericho.

Below: Jericho, the Mt. of Temptation

Above: Hisham's Palace, Jericho.
Opposite: St. George's Monastery, Wadi Kelt

HISHAM'S PALACE

The Moslem Ummayad Caliph Hisham ibn Abd-el-Malik built a sumptuous winter palace during the eighth century. It was destroyed by an earthquake four years later. It consisted of a pillared courtyard, two mosques and two bath houses with beautiful mosaic floors. Perhaps one of the best preserved and most beautiful mosaics in the land is to be seen at Hisham's Palace. Carved stone remains found in the complex give some idea of how impressive the palace must have been.

Above: Qumran - the caves where the Dead Sea Scrolls were discovered

Below: Part of the Habbakuk Commentary - one of the Seven Dead Sea Scrolls housed in the Shrine of the Book in Jerusalem

QUMRAN

The most stunning biblical archaeological find took place in 1947, when a young Beduin boy un- knowingly discovered a hoard of ancient manu- scripts, the Dead Sea Scrolls high up in a cave at Qumran, on the western shore of the Dead Sea. Excavations led by Roland de Vaux have uncovered remains from five periods when the settlement of Qumran was inhabited.

The vast scriptorium bears evidence of the scribes' work - transcribing texts from the Bible and other works written during the Second Temple era on leather, papyrus and copper.

When Titus and the Roman legions arrived at Jericho, the Essenes, as the sect was known, fled, hiding their scrolls in the nearby caves. The desert kept their secret for almost 2,000 years. The discovery of the scrolls had an enormous effect on the Christian world, as they were transcribed during the time of the birth of Christianity. The scrolls which were discovered at Qumran are now housed in the Shrine of the Book at the Israel Museum in Jerusalem.

Above: *Ruins of the Scriptorium*
Below: *The entrance to one of the caves discovered in the summer of 1952*

EIN FESHKA

The natural fresh water pools of Ein Feshka are being developed into a popular bathing complex. The whole Dead Sea area has fast become a holidaymaker's paradise - offering something to suit all tastes.

The adventurous can now enjoy rappelling down the steep desert cliffs. Camel safaris and off-the-beaten-track jeep tours are all available. The perfect climate with warm sunshine and mineral-rich air are added factors in favour of Israel's newest centre for relaxation and fun.

Above right: On the way to the Dead Sea
Below right: Rappelling in the Judean cliffs. A popular sport for the energetic
Below left: The oasis of Ein Feshka by the Dead Sea

EIN GEDI

The biblical oasis of Ein Gedi lies near the shores of the Dead Sea. It was one of the desert settlements of the Tribe of Judah. David fled from King Saul to Ein Gedi. Famous for its springs and waterfalls the lush tropical vegetation is the perfect setting for the ibex and occasional leopard that still roam freely in this beautiful nature reserve.

Kibbutz Ein Gedi, established in 1949, has developed into a holiday and study centre. Tourism and the growing of dates provide income for the members. The field school with its guest house is always busy. Holidaymakers enjoy the facilities and informality of these "down-to-earth" comfortable lodgings provided by the hostels and camping sites in the area. For those with more sophisticated tastes there are hotels of all grades further along the sea shore at Ein Bokek.

Left: Nahal David - the waterfall at Ein Gedi
Below right: Ibex in the nature reserve at Ein Gedi

MASADA

The heroic stand of the zealots at Masada in 73 A.D. is probably the most well known story in the long history of Israel. Herod's stronghold is set on a wide plateau overlooking the Dead Sea.

A few coins minted during the reign of Alexander Jannaeus (103-76 B.C.) were found during excavations at Masada. These are all that remain from this king's reign.

In 40 B.C. Herod fled from Jerusalem, taking refuge with his wife and family at Masada. Leaving them there he continued on his journey to Egypt, finally reaching Rome. Chosen to be king of Judea in 37 B.C. Herod returned to Masada together with two Roman legions. He built himself huge palaces with wonderful mosaic floors and magnificently decorated walls. Enormous storehouses and massive

Opposite: Aerial view of Masada
Above left:
Close-up showing the wall paintings on the lower terrace of Herod's Palace
Below: The store rooms

fortifications were also added to the complex. When Herod died in 4 B.C. Masada passed to his son, Archelaus, but soon it was taken over by Roman rule.

Masada became an armed Jewish encampment when it was taken over by zealots in 66 A.D. Many survivors fled from Jerusalem after its fall in 70 A.D. Taking refuge atop Masada they banded together holding out against Rome until 72 A.D. when the Tenth Roman Legion started to attack this final Jewish stronghold. The zealots held out for another year until 73 A.D. when they chose to commit mass suicide rather than be captured by their enemy.

Maintained once more as a Roman garrison Masada soon fell into disuse, until it was inhabited for a short while by a small band of Byzantine monks during the fifth century.

Deserted once more Masada remained silent and unused until the inception of the State of Israel. Now it is the venue for the solemn swearing-in ceremony of soldiers from one of Israel's elite armoured units. With the words: "Masada shall not fall again!" ringing in their ears, they carry on the tradition of the zealots.

Opposite:
Above left: *The Caldarium in the bath house*
Above right: *Herod's Northern palace showing middle and lower terraces.*
Below left: *The synagogue*
Below right: *The Western gate*

THE DEAD SEA

The Dead Sea is the lowest spot on earth, 1,290 feet below sea level. Containing 30% of magnesium, sodium, calcium, potassium chloride and other salts, it has the highest mineral content of any body of water in the world. These salts are refined at the Dead Sea Works and used for agricultural and industrial purposes - both locally and abroad. Mounds of crystallized salt formations dot the shoreline looming out of the water like eerie sentinels. Nothing grows in the immediate area. Animal life, as we know it, is impossible; hence its name, the Dead Sea.

The black mud found in vast quantities has scientifically recognized curative qualities. Bathing in the natural sulphur pools, or just floating on the oily water are both helpful to people suffering from skin diseases or muscular problems.

The Dead Sea Health Spa is a modern, well equipped centre providing many facilities for different treatments. The excellent hotels ensure comfort and relaxation for both tourists and locals who wish to stay in this rapidly expanding health resort.

Previous page - Above - right: The Columbarium.
Previous page - Centre - right: The Swimming pool.
Previous page - Below - left: Stoves and Silos in the tower of the western wall.
Previous page - Below right: One of the enormous cisterns which Herod's engineers carved out of the solid rock.

Below: Resort hotels at the Dead Sea shore.
opposite:
Above left: Crystallized salt "mushroom".
Above right: Fun with mud from the Dead Sea
Below left: Floating on the Dead Sea

SODOM

Sodom, at the southern tip of the Dead Sea, is associated with the Bible (Genesis 19:24).

Lot and his wife, fleeing to Zoar from the doomed city of Sodom, were warned not to look back to their city which was to be destroyed by fire and brimstone, because of the wickedness of its people. Lot's wife disobeyed, looked backwards, and was turned into a pillar of salt. On the slopes of Mount Sodom there stands to this day a pillar of salt - which, with a little imagination, could well be Lot's wife.

The grey salt rocks and canyons of the Sodom region are indeed barren and cursed.

Above: The Pillar of Salt - Lot's wife, Sodom
Below: Canyons in the salt rock mountains of Sodom
Opposite:
Above left: Beersheba - modern shopping centre
Below: Ben Gurion University of the Negev

BEERSHEBA

Beersheba, the capital of the Negev, has expanded at a tremendous rate. Modern architecture can be seen in the well-planned Ben Gurion University of the Negev, the University Hospital, the shopping complex in the town centre and the municipal buildings.

Houses and schools are designed to withstand the heat and dryness of the desert days, and the drop in temperature at night.

The market held every Thursday morning is a noisy meeting place for Beduin from far and wide. Gathering here they trade livestock and produce. Tourists love to come and see this colourful sight. They also enjoy purchasing souvenirs. The choice is endless - glassware, pottery, carved wood, long-stemmed pipes and numerous objects of brassware and metal are all readily available. Bartering for a bargain is half the fun of the market. Usually a smile and a handshake close a deal - leaving both the salesman and the customer happy.

Opposite: Scenes from the Beduin market at Beersheba
Above: Ashdod - the modern town
Below: Ashkelon - ancient ruins in the National Park

ASHDOD

Situated on the Mediterranean coast, Ashdod was built in 1957. It is centred around Israel's largest and newest port which was originally planned chiefly for the export of citrus fruit. Today it is a busy, thriving town with dock facilities and an electric power station.

Ancient Ashdod was a major Canaanite town set along the Via Maris. Later it became one of the five Philistine cities.

ASHKELON

A little further south is the modern holiday resort town of Ashkelon. It is thought to have been the birthplace of Herod the Great. The National Park contains many of the columns, capitals and statues of ancient Ashkelon.

TEL-AVIV

Tel-Aviv was the first Jewish town to be established in Israel in modern times. Starting off in 1909 as a suburb of Jaffa, it is now Israel's second largest city, after Jerusalem.

Tel-Aviv is the commercial capital of Israel. Major industrial and commercial concerns have their headquarters here. The political party headquarters are also found in Tel-Aviv. Cultural activities abound in this noisy, bustling city. It is the home of the world renowned Israel Philharmonic Orchestra. Two universities serve the metropolis, Tel-Aviv University and Bar-Ilan University in nearby Ramat Gan. For the museum lover there are two major places to visit - the Tel-Aviv Museum and the Diaspora Museum.

Hotels, restaurants and cafes are available in all price ranges to suit all pockets. The busy streets are crowded with shoppers, there is something to suit all tastes.

The modern tendency to move out of the big city and into the suburbs has not escaped Tel-Aviv.

Consequently its population is slowly shrinking and ageing. However, the glitter and grime, the culture and coarseness which make up Tel-Aviv guarantee it a life and dynamism all of its own.

Above: Old Jaffa - aerial view towards Tel-Aviv
The harbour and marina, Jaffa
Opposite: Tel-Aviv - bird's eye view

Overleaf p.74
Above left: Carmel market, Tel Aviv
Above right: Bet Hatefutsot, the Diaspora Museum
Below: Tel Aviv's skyline seen from the sea
Overleaf p.75
Above left: Ramat Aviv mall
Above right: Azrieli center
Below: Neve Zedek quarter with Tel Aviv's "City" in the background

OLD JAFFA

Biblical Joppa was named after Japhet, the son of Noah. An ancient Canaanite city and port, it has many associations with the Bible. The story of Jonah and the whale is connected with Jaffa. Here Jonah set off on his journey to Tarshish (Jonah 1:17). Solomon imported cedars from Lebanon which were unloaded at Jaffa and taken to Jerusalem to build the Temple.

A group of Jewish settlers in Jaffa moved away and founded Tel-Aviv in 1909. The new city expanded quickly and soon became the noisy, busy commercial and entertainment centre of Israel. The two cities united into a single municipality in 1950.

From ancient Jaffa the coastline of modern Tel-Aviv is clearly visible. The palms and relative serenity of Jaffa give way to high-rise concrete buildings.

Aerial view of Old Jaffa

Jaffa offers all the modern tourist facilities, together with the quaint charm of the artists' quarter, where one can browse amongst works of art of all kinds and at all prices. Superb restaurants, many specializing in preparing locally caught fish, and a gay night life complete the tourists' day.

NETANYA

On the shores of the Mediterranean Sea, Netanya has developed into one of Israel's foremost resort towns. Hotels, pensions and private homes offer all types of accommodation to the holidaymaker. Beautiful stretches of golden sand make this the ideal venue for family holidays.

Above: Old Jaffa at night. The multi-media show, "The Israel Experience" is a popular tourist attraction.
Below: Old Jaffa at night with the church of St. Peter in the upper part of the picture.

Above: *Netanya, the beach: bird's eye view, with high-rise apartment buildings and hotels in the background*
Below left: *Caesarea, the golf course and club house*

CAESAREA

Built by Herod on the shores of the Mediterranean and named after Caesar Augustus. Caesarea was one of the most splendid cities of the ancient world, filled with all the luxuries that constituted Graeco-Roman culture. Excavations have revealed the remains of a hippodrome, and amphitheatre, a theatre and hot baths.

Today Caesarea is visited daily by tourists from Israel and abroad who come to marvel at the Crusader fortress, the Byzantine statues and the marketplace.

There is a golf course, hotel and many luxurious vil-

Above: *Excavations at ancient Caesarea*
Below: *The Roman theatre at Caesarea*

las in modern Caesarea, all testifying to the wealth and development of this old/new seaside town. Restaurants and cafes provide excellent meals and refreshments for those who wish to relax by the sea.

Haifa - view from Mount Carmel. The golden domed Bahai Shrine in the foreground

HAIFA

The city is built above the harbour on the slopes of Mount Carmel. The landscape is dominated by the gold-plated dome of the Bahai Temple set in formal Persian gardens. This is the centre of the Bahai faith which stresses the unity of God and the brotherhood of mankind.

Haifa is Israel's third largest city after Tel-Aviv and Jerusalem. Building the Hejaz railway line in 1905, the construction of the harbour in 1933 and the refineries in 1934 all helped in the rapid development of Haifa.

The city was destroyed by the Crusaders and rebuilt by a Beduin ruler during the 18th century. From the Carmel range above the city there is a wonderful panoramic view. The port is always busy; ships large and small wait outside the breakwater for their turn to unload goods, or luxury liners wait for passengers to disembark.

Grain silos, warehouses and the Haifa refineries are all along the quays. All the facilities needed for the maintenance of ships are available.

The red roofed houses once belonged to the German Templar Colony. Haifa University and the Technion turn out highly qualified and skilled engineers and scholars in many fields.

Pre-historic man once lived in the caves of the Carmel. The range is mentioned a few times in the Bible as a place of beauty, and as a place of worship and retreat. This is indeed true of the Carmellite Monastery where tranquility reigns supreme.

A cave under the monastery is believed to be the refuge of Elijah when he hid from Ahab - according to Jewish tradition, however, this cave is further down the mountain.

A statue of Elijah stands in the grounds of the Carmellite Monastery at Mukhraka. This marks the spot where Elijah slew the false prophets of Baal.

Haifa is home to several small but interesting museums - the Maritime Museum, Naval and Illegal Immigration Museum, Museum of Antiquities, & Museum of Modern Art and the Museum of Japanese Art.

Near Haifa, on the heights of Mt. Carmel, are the picturesque Druze villages of Daliat el-Carmel and Issafia with their large range of Druze arts and crafts in the main streets.

Above: Haifa, the Bahai terraced gardens
Below: Stella Maris monastery

Overleaf:
Above right: Haifa at night
Above left: The statue of Elijah at Muhraka on Mt. Carmel
Below: Bird's eye view of Haifa with Mt. Carmel in the foreground

THE JEZREEL VALLEY

The Jezreel Valley is the largest valley in Israel, cutting the country in two between Galilee and Samaria. The valley was the natural route for the passage of armies and caravans from the coastal plain to the Jordan Valley.

The entire area was a malarial swamp until the land was reclaimed by Jewish settlers. Malaria was slowly eradicated, and the valley became green and fertile. Today it is populated by kibbutzim and guest houses, and provides a high percentage of the country's fruits, vegetables and farm produce.

Above left: *Jezreel Valley and Givat Hamoreh*
Below: *Megiddo - excavations at the ancient tel*

MEGIDDO

Megiddo is situated on the Via Maris. It was a major battleground in the past because of its strategic location and importance - connecting the towns in the centre of the country with the sea. It is related in the New Testament that Armageddon (Megiddo) is where the final battle between the forces of good and evil will take place.

Megiddo was one of the walled city-states taken by Joshua. Excavations carried out in 1925 revealed twenty cities superimposed one on top of the other at the Megiddo tel. The oldest of these cities dates back to 4,000 B.C.

Remains can be seen of a partially restored walled town with superb gates. Excellent models explain the complicated archaeological complex.

An underground water tunnel linked the inhabitants to the water source located beyond the walls. A Canaanite temple, palaces, storehouses, sentry towers and soldiers' quarters were all contained within the walls.

Above right: Megiddo, the water tunnel leading to the spring
Below right: Canaanite altar
Below left: Steps beneath the town's Solomonic gateway

ACRE

In the Bible we learn that Acre and its surroundings fell to the lot of Asher after Joshua overran Canaan and divided it up among the Children of Israel. The Canaanites and the Asherites lived together in this thriving sea port on the Via Maris which was established some 4,000 years ago. Acre is mentioned in the Amarna letters, always referred to as a prosperous sea port.

In 333 B.C.E. it was granted permission to mint its own coins. Renamed Ptolemais, it continued to thrive. It became an army headquarters under the Romans who launched their attacks against the Jewish strongholds in Galilee. Acre was ruled by the Crusaders and then the Mamelukes. In 1775 Ahmed el-Jazzar built the Great Mosque with its marble pillars and elaborate decorations. This distinctive landmark can be seen for miles around. The hot baths, now turned into the Municipal Museum, were also erected by el-Jazzar.

Opposite the mosque, under the Turkish Citadel, are the enormous halls built by the Crusaders. Today concerts are held in the Knights' Hall - a unique underground experience.

Acre - bird's eye view.

Acre was included in the British Mandate of 1918. With the Declaration of Independence in 1948 it started to develop and expand. The colourful oriental bazaar, the port, the old city walls, the cannons and the ancient churches are all waiting to be visited and explored. Annual festivals for music, theatre and dance are a new attraction.

Above left: Khan El Uumdan with clock tower
Above right: Interior of the Municipal Museum
Below: Acre seen from the sea
Opposite:
Above right: The Mosque of El Jazar
Above left: Interior of the Mosque
Below right: The market
Below left: St. John's Crypt

ROSH HANIKRA

Natural grottos at Rosh Hanikra have been formed by the constant action of the sea against the white chalk cliffs. This point on the Israel-Lebanon border has now become a favourite tourist attraction. Kibbutz Lohamei Hageta'ot closeby adjoins part of the Turkish aqueduct which once carried water from the Spring of Kabri to Acre.

Above left: *Nahariya, Gaaton Avenue*
Below: *Rosh Hanikra - entrance to the grottos*

Above: Aerial view of Safed. In the background, Mt. Meron.
Below: The Joseph Caro Synagogue, Safed

SAFED

The capital of Upper Galilee, Safed, is perched 3,000 feet above sea level, high up on a mountain top. The wonderful views from every narrow lane and alleyway, the crisp mountain air and the mystical setting all combine to make this a popular holiday venue. Painters, sculptors and craftsmen are drawn to the renovated Artists' Quarter where many have workshops and galleries.

During the War of Independence Safed was the scene of a furious battle. Miraculously the outnumbered Jewish citizens won. The Davidka - a small gun that makes a lot of noise - still stands in the main street as a memorial to the fallen of this battle.

Safed is the home of mysticism (Kabbala) which developed here in the 16th century under the leadership of Rabbi Isaac Luria. The first Hebrew printing press in the Middle East was set up here in 1563.

ZIPPORI (SEPPHORIS)

Near Nazareth is the archaeological site of Zippori, which Josephus described as "the greatest city in all Galilee". It was built by Antipas, son of Herod, to serve as administrative center of the region and later gained prominence as the seat of the Sanhedrin, the Jewish Council. It is traditionally the birthplace of Mary, mother of Jesus, and Joseph and Jesus may well have worked here as carpenters.

Archaeologists have excavated a 4000-seat Roman theater, numerous streets laid out in grid formation and an impressive rock-hewn water system. Many magnificent mosaics have been unearthed, and the beautiful third-century CE Dionysian floor in a reconstructed Roman villa has been called the "Mona Lisa of the Galilee". There are also remains of 12th century Crusader fortifications; from here the Crusaders marched to their crushing defeat by Saladdin at the Horns of Hittim in 1187.

Left: Reconstructed scene of daily life in the first century at Sepphoris
Below right: The "Mona Lisa of the Galilee"; detail of mosaic floor
Below left: Part of the Cardo at Sepphoris

NAZARETH

The city of Nazareth is located in a valley in southern Galilee. It was here that Joseph and his wife, Mary, lived, and Jesus spent his childhood.

In the first centuries A.D. Nazareth was populated only by Jews, but with the strengthening of the Roman Empire, the number of Christians living there grew. From the fourth century onwards, churches were built on the sites which were connected with Jesus and the Virgin Mary.

Today the population of Nazareth is a mixture of Christians, Moslems and Jews. The Christians belong to various denominations: Orthodox, Roman Catholic, Greek Catholic, Maronite, Anglican, Copt, Armenian, Baptist and other Protestant sects. There are many churches, monasteries, convents, hostels, hospitals and schools maintained by the various denominations.

Every view of Nazareth is dominated by the Basilica of the Annunciation. The present Basilica, which was designed by the Italian architect, Prof. Giovanni Muzio, was completed in 1969. It is the fifth church built on the spot where the Angel Gabriel stood when he prophesied to the Virgin Mary that she would conceive a child. Remains of the first church were discovered during excavations which were started on the site in 1955. The second church was built during the Byzantine period; the third at the beginning of the 12th century and the fourth was completed in 1877.

Nazareth, general view

MARY'S WELL

Spring water is carried by an aqueduct to Mary's Well, close to St. Gabriel's Church. Today, as in biblical times, the water is drawn in clay jars from the ornamental fountain, and carried away by donkeys.

THE CHURCH OF ST. GABRIEL

Close to Mary's well is the Church of St. Gabriel. Built by the Crusaders in the 12th century the original church marked the place where it is traditionally believed that the Angel Gabriel first appeared to Mary. In 1781 the Greek Orthodox community built the present church.

Above left: The Church of the Annunciation
Above right: The Grotto of the Annunciation
Below left: Interior of the Church of the Annunciation
Opposite:
Above right: Entrance to the Greek Orthodox Church of St. Gabriel
Above left: Mary's well
Below left: The Grotto of the Holy Family
Below right: Market scene

KFAR CANA

The little village of Kfar Cana, close to Nazareth is identified as the site where Jesus performed His first miracle of converting water into wine at a wedding. His mother and His disciples were guests at the feast. A painting hanging above the altar in the small church shows Jesus at the wedding.

The present church, known as the Church of the Miracle, is constructed on the ruins of a church built in the sixth century A.D. Inside there is a mosaic floor from the fourth century. Many young couples come here to celebrate their weddings. In the crypt of the church a Roman water jug symbolizes the larger ones used to hold water at the time of the first miracle.

Above right: *Interior of the Church of the Miracle at Cana*
Below: *Kfar Cana*

MOUNT TABOR

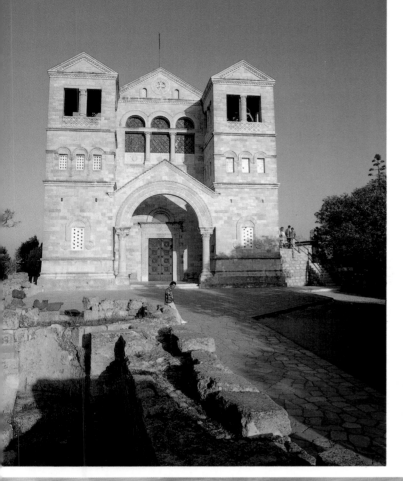

The rounded mountain in the Jezreel Valley is of great importance to Christians. This is the traditional place of the transfiguration of Jesus. Commemorating this event a modern church was built at the summit in 1924 by the architect Antonio Barluzzi in the Roman-Syrian style of the 4th - 7th centuries. The remains of previous basilicas were discovered in the construction.

Above the 12th century Crusader altar of the central apse in the Basilica of the Transfiguration is a golden mosaic representing the transfiguration. Jesus is the central figure surrounded by the prophets Moses and Elijah. Depicted below them are Peter, James and John. He was transfigured by them, his face shining like the sun, and his clothing brilliant white.

Above: *Mount Tabor, the Basilica of the Transfiguration*
Below: *Mount Tabor*

TIBERIAS

The capital of the Lower Galilee, Tiberias is situated 209 metres below sea level on the southwest shore of the Sea of Galilee. Herod Antipas, the son of Herod the Great, founded the town in about 20 A.D.

Many of the Gospel stories took place around this area of Galilee.

Today the biblical atmosphere of tranquility has been replaced by the noise and gaiety of a modern tourist resort. The hot mineral springs of nearby Hamat Tiberias are as popular now as they were in Roman times.

Water sports are another attraction as the mild winter temperatures make it possible to enjoy this activity all the year round. Good hotels, restaurants and beaches are all added inducements for the visitor today in Tiberias.

Below: General view of Tiberias, showing the hotel complex
Above: Tiberias, looking towards south, the archaeological garden in the foreground.

Above left: Tiberias - the pilgrim boats
Above right: Remains of the Church of Mt. Bereniki
Below: Mosaic floor at Hamat Synagogue

MOUNT ARBEL

The high cliffs of Mount Arbel overlook the western shore of the Sea of Galilee. This was the site of a battle in 39 B.C.E. between the zealots living in the caves and Herod's warriors. The story is told by Josephus of a family who killed themselves rather than be taken captive.

Above: Mt. Arbel - bird's eye view
Below: Kibbutz Nof Ginossar
Opposite: The Jordan Valley
Below: The Ancient Galilee Boat

KIBBUTZ GINNOSAR

The Kibbutz on the shores of the Sea of Galilee, has a well run guest house providing a good base for touring the surrounding countryside.

The Galilee boat, an ancient fishing vessel, was discovered on the shores of the lake during the drought year of 1985. It is now housed in the Beit Allon Museum - a new cultural centre for the preservation of archaeological finds from the area.

THE ANCIENT GALILEE BOAT

The discovery in 1986 of this ancient vessel, mired in the mud near Magdala on the northwest shore of the Sea of Galilee, caused a stir throughout the world, especially after it was conclusively dated to the fateful first century CE, the time both of Jesus and the Great Revolt of the Jews against the Romans. The boat, made primarily of cedar and oak, is now on exhibit at Kibbutz Ginnosar. It is 9 meters long, 2.5 meters wide, and 1.25 meters high. It may have functioned as a ferry boat, but its measurements also suit use by ancient fishermen employing a seine, or dragnet, "cast into the sea" as described in Matt 13:47-48.

YARDENIT

Near to Kibbutz Degania Aleph, where the River Jordan leaves the Sea of Galilee, we find Yardenit - the Place of Baptism. Pilgrims gather here from all over the world. Clad in white robes they immerse themselves in the holy waters of the River Jordan. With devout sincerity they believe that they are following in the tradition of the scriptures.

EIN GEV

The kibbutz of Ein Gev on the east bank of the Kinneret was founded in 1939. Once threatened by Syrian forces it is today a flourishing community. Fishing is still the main livelihood of the members, supplemented by the produce from the date plantations and banana groves. The popular fish restaurant is a "must" for all tourists, whilst the annual spring music festival is becoming world famous.

Yardenit, the place of Baptism.

HAMAT GADER

Since the time of the Second Temple, Hamat Gader has been well known for its hot springs. Excavations that began in 1979 have uncovered well preserved Roman baths, pottery, coins and glass artifacts. Holidaymakers can spend a pleasant day relaxing in the bathing pools that are filled with hot water from the springs. An added attraction are the pools amongst the trees and tall grasses, where alligators imported from Florida bask lazily in the sun.

Above: Ein Gev - with Mt. Susita in the background
Below left: Hamat Gader - the Roman baths
Below right: Hamat Gader - a crocodile

CAPERNAUM

In Roman days Capernaum was a prosperous Jewish town situated on a major highway. Excavations have revealed remains of a synagogue from the fourth century. This probably stands on the site of the original synagogue in which Jesus preached, healed the sick, and performed many miracles during his ministry in Galilee. The beautifully carved white limestone decorations with many Jewish symbols are in sharp contrast to the simple black basalt homes nearby.

An octagonal church from the fifth century was built over what is believed to be the house of Peter. A circular church has now been erected over this traditional site and the remains of the Byzantine church.

Millstones and an olive press lie abandoned close to the family living quarters and the new church.

Fishing in the sparkling blue waters of the Sea of Galilee is still an important occupation as it was in biblical times.

TABGHA

The simple church built in the fourth century commemorates one of the most well known miracles that Jesus performed.

The new Church at Tabgha was built over the remains of a fourth century church which itself was built on an earlier church with a beautiful mosaic floor. The mosaic commemorates - the "feeding of the multitude" with five loaves and two fishes. Water birds, local flora and other motifs are also depicted in the mosaics. Like the original building, the church is a large basilica with three naves. The grounds belong to the German Catholic Committee which was responsible for the excavations.

The church was built next to ancient steps leading down to the waterline.

Above: *The exterior of the Church of the Loaves and the Fishes*
Below: *The mosaic of the Loaves and the Fishes, Tabgha*

THE MOUNT OF BEATITUDES

Situated atop the Mount of Beatitudes overlooking the Sea of Galilee the octagonal shaped chapel of the Church of the Beatitudes marks the spot where Jesus delivered the Sermon of the Mount (Matthew 5:3 - 10).

Antonio Barluzzi built the church in 1937. Colonnaded cloisters surround the entire structure offering a beautiful panoramic view of the Sea of Galilee.

On each window of the cupola is written part of the text of the eight Beatitudes, as spoken by Jesus when he delivered his Sermon on the Mount. (Matthew 5:3 - 10).

CHURCH OF ST. PETER'S PRIMACY

The church was built next to ancient steps leading down to the waterline.

Opposite: *The Church of the Beatitudes*
Below: *The Church of St. Peter's Primacy, Tabgha*

HAZOR

The important biblical site of Hazor was probably the largest of the Canaanite city-states. During the time of the Israelite conquest it was a stronghold of considerable size and importance. The tel is composed of two sections - the higher, more strongly defended acropolis, and a lower city fortified by a compressed earthern rampart.

METULLA

On the Lebanese border, Metulla is developing rapidly into a popular tourist resort. The once sleepy little town now boasts a thriving sports centre sponsored by the people of Canada. International competitions and exhibitions are planned to take place at the modern indoor skating rink.

Above left: *Tel Hazor with Kibbutz Ayelet Hashahar in the background*

Below: *Manara cliff cable-car, view towards Kiryat Shemona*
Opposite:
Above: *Aerial view of Metulla.*

Below right: *The River Jordan. In the background, snow-capped Mount Hermon*
Below left: *The Trumpeldor memorial at Tel-Hai*

BANIAS

The spring of Banias is one of the three sources of the River Jordan. A Hellenistic town was once built here for the Greek god Pan. The votary niche in the temple to the god overlooks lush greenery and bubbling rivulets. The Banias waterfall nearby adds to the beauty of this peaceful setting.

Opposite:
Above: The Banias waterfall
Below left: Nimrod Castle (Kala'at Namrud) a Crusader fortress on the slopes of Mount Hermon
Below right: Votary niche in the Temple of Pan at Banias
The Hulah Valley. In the background, the Golan Heights
Insert: At the Hula Nature Reserve

THE GOLAN HEIGHTS

The Golan Heights rise above the fertile Hulah Valley which is closely cultivated. Mt. Hermon is usually capped with snow. From 1948-1967 the kibbutzim in the valley were constantly threatened by fire from the Syrian army which was installed on the mountains. The Six Day War finally ended this threat. Settlements have sprung up on the Heights - mostly agricultural, they are thriving on the fertile soil of the volcanic mountains.

Remains of the Syrian bunkers and fortifications can still be seen. During the Six Day War, most of the Moslem inhabitants fled, but the Druze remained and continue to tend their apple orchards.

MOUNT HERMON

Snow-capped Mt. Hermon is the highest spot in Israel. Mentioned in the Bible in the Book of Joshua, Mount Hermon is rapidly becoming a well run ski site with first class facilities. A holiday resort village on the slopes, it is especially popular in winter when guests enjoy skiing - using the chair-lift to take them to the summit.

At the juncture of the Hermon and the Golan Heights is a deep, almost perfectly round pool of very blue water. Called Birkat Ram, this strange phenomenon, with no visible inlet or outlet for the mass of water, is the subject of many imaginative stories and legends.

KATZRIN

There was a Jewish settlement at Katzrin almost 2,000 years ago. Proof of this is the remains of an ornately decorated synagogue found in the area.

Today Katzrin is a thriving town in the Golan - apartment buildings, libraries, community centres and a modern shopping centre cater to the needs of the fast growing community.

Among the sites worth visiting are the synagogue and model of an ancient village, the Museum and the winery where grapes from the area are made into the gourmet Gamla and Golan wines.

Above: *Ski resort - Mount Hermon*
Below: *Birkat Ram*
Below right: *Reconstructed ovens at ancient Katzrin*

GAMLA

The story of Gamla is similar to that of Masada - in fact Gamla is sometimes called the Masada of the North. In 68 C.E. many hundreds of the defenders of Gamla killed themselves and their families rather than being captured by the approaching Romans. The ruins of a first century C.E. synagogue have been uncovered at the zealot fortress of Gamla. Today pioneer families have settled in the area.

Above: *Katzrin - the ancient synagogue*
Below: *Gamla - the famous fortress on the Golan Heights*

BEIT SHEAN

This was an important town until the late Middle Ages. Eighteen layers of cities have been unearthed by archaeologists - the Roman layer probably being the most impressive. A superb amphitheatre, wide streets adorned with marble columns, and the largest Roman theatre in the country have all been revealed at this fascinating archaeological site.

The development town of Beit Shean is being transformed from a sleepy backwater to a prominent tourist attraction as the reconstruction of the great Roman town goes forward by leaps and bounds.

Opposite:
Above: *Beit Shean excavations*
Below: *Beit Shean - The Roman theatre*
Beit Shean - bird's eye view

Above: The Sde Boker Academy (Midrasha) in the Negev
Insert: The grave of David Ben-Gurion,
Israel's first Prime Minister
Below: Ein Avdat canyon

SDE BOKER

One year after the setting up of Kibbutz Sde Boker David Ben Gurion decided to live there together with his wife, Paula. Israel's first prime minister had planned a great future for the Negev. His vision of agricultural and industrial development has only been partially fulfilled. The Sde Boker Academy (Midrasha) is perhaps his greatest lasting achievement in the Negev. He and his wife, Paula, are buried in simple graves overlooking the wilderness of Zin. Throughout the year many people come to pay homage to this great man.

EIN AVDAT

Close to Sde Boker is the Avdat Canyon which leads to Ein Avdat The narrow ravine of sheer white cliffs provides an exciting walk. One is rewarded by the sight of the clear water, icy cold in spite of the hot desert sun.

AVDAT

Avdat is the first of the Nabatean towns to be restored. The ancient ruins reveal the wonderful town planning that was practised so many years ago. In particular the Nabateans had a most remarkable system for water collection, storage and irrigation. Scientists have been experimenting - trying to copy their system and make the desert bloom.

THE RAMON CRATER

At the Visitors' Centre of Mitzpeh Ramon, with the help of pictures, audio-visual programmes and models, youngsters and adults are introduced to some of the secrets of the Negev and begin to appreciate the wonders of geology.

Trails have been marked out in the huge Park Ramon Nature Reserve.

This picture of the Ramon Crater is taken from one of the viewpoints along one of these trails.

Above: *Ancient ruins at Avdat*
Below: *The Ramon Crater*

TIMNA PARK

Kibbutz Elot has opened a desert park, a new nature reserve protecting the ancient copper mines, an excavated Eygptian Temple of Hathor and the remarkable stone "Mushroom".

SOLOMON'S PILLARS

The huge red sandstone rocks, known as Solomon's Pillars, stand at the entrance to the Timna mines, which have produced copper on and off for 6,000 years. Surrounded by breathtaking scenery these pillars are well worth taking time to visit.

Opposite: *Eilat - the marina on the Red Sea*
Above: *King Solomon's Pillars*
Below: *Timna Valley Park*

Above: *The Coral World Underwater Observatory*
Below: *The coast of Eilat*

EILAT

Eilat is well known today as the place where the winter is always sunny and mild. Thousands of vacationers come to Eilat every year, travelling by land, sea and air. They come to enjoy a relaxing holiday with swimming, sunbathing and water sports.

Modern hotels, pensions and rooms in private houses are all available to suit every taste.

Shopping arcades restaurants, cafes, bars and discotheques are all geared to tourism. The cosmopolitan atmosphere of Eilat today is one of its great assets.

In a few short years Eilat has grown tremendously. New roads serve the city; social services, schools and medical services have all improved. Inland flights from Eilat to Tel-Aviv and Jerusalem are a popular method of quick carefree travel.

Today Eilat is a thriving, dynamic community with the second generation taking over the reins from their pioneering parents. The government of Israel, having recognized the importance of the town's major industry - international tourism, has declared

119

Eilat to be a free trade zone, paving the way for even greater enlargement and development of the Red Sea port.

CORAL WORLD UNDERWATER OBSERVATORY AQUARIUM

Perhaps one of the biggest attractions in this resort town today is the Coral World Underwater Observatory and Aquarium. Many years of expert biological research, planning and building were needed before the project was completed and the doors opened to the public. Here the visitor can see the splendours of underwater life in the Red Sea in air-conditioned comfort. The breathtakingly beautiful colours and shapes of the thousands of tropical fish and invertebrates that pass through the observatory enthral the visitor and also aid marine scientists in their studies of the coral reef environment.

Left: The Underwater Observatory and the Yellow Submarin

Underwater scenery in the Red Sea

Above: *Diving in the Red Sea*
Below: *Dolphin Reef*

DIVING IN THE RED SEA

The Coral Beach - south of Eilat - is the venue for scuba diving or snorkeling. Here the seas are still unpolluted and the temperature of the water is almost constant throughout the year. The Nature Reserves Authority guards the coastline carefully - the rich and colourful flora and fauna are preserved. It is forbidden to take corals or shells out of the sea, and fishing is only allowed at certain spots along the shore.

THE DOLPHIN REEF

A unique way of spending a day is with the dolphins in their natural habitat. An area in the Red Sea has been fenced off so that holiday-makers and these friendly mammals can consort together in complete safety. The Dolphin Reef is also an ideal venue for open-air concerts on summer nights.

Opposite:
above:: *Jules Verne, explorer, mobile undersea observatory, Eilat.*
below: *Divers on their way to the Red Sea.*
Above Left: *The Red Canion*
Above right: *The Amram pillars*
Below right: *Desert view*

TOURS FROM EILAT

As well as having sunshine all year round, Eilat is a convenient base for trips to many places of interest. At the Timna Valley Park, situated 30 kms north of Eilat, one can marvel at the ancient technologies and rock carvings, visit the remains of the Temple to Hathor, see rare rock formations and the famous Solomons Pillars. Also north of Eilat is the Chai Bar Nature Reserve which aims to bring back to the area animals recorded in the Bible as indigenous. Other beautiful trips are to Ein Netafim and the Red Canyon and other desert tours which the adventurous can make on the back of a camel.

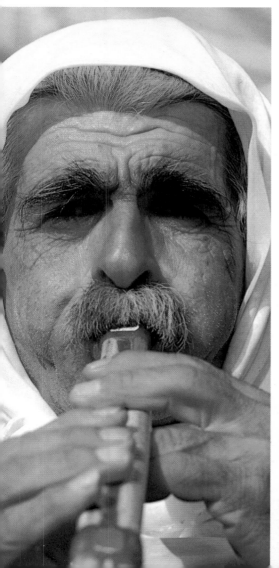

INDEX